A Pilgrimage

to

Dartmoor's Crosses

A Pilgrimage

to

Dartmoor's Crosses

By Tim Sandles

FOREST PUBLISHING

First published in 1997 by FOREST PUBLISHING, Woodstock, Liverton, Newton Abbot, Devon TQ12 6JJ

British Library Cataloguing in Publication Data

A catalogue record for this book is available from the British Library.

ISBN 0–9527297–3–3

Forest Publishing

Editorial, design and layout by:
Mike & Karen Lang

Typeset by:
Carnaby Typesetting, Torquay, Devon TQ1 1EG

Printed and bound in Great Britain by:
BPC Wheatons Ltd., Exeter, Devon EX2 8RP

Cover illustrations:

Cross at Lower Dunstone, near Widecombe-in-the-Moor.

DEDICATION

This book is dedicated to Irene and to my father, Ernest Sandles.

CONTENTS

ACKNOWLEDGEMENTS

I would like to offer my sincere thanks to Irene, for her help on many of the visits to the crosses; to Mike and Karen Lang, for their assistance and co-operation with the editorial aspect of this book; and to Mike Wallsh, for his companionship on several research trips.

PREFACE

The crosses included in this book are all sited within, or very close to, the boundary of the Dartmoor National Park as defined by the Ordnance Survey maps.

Only some of them, however, are actually shown on the O.S. maps, and even then not always entirely accurately. As a result, a six-figure grid reference has been provided for each cross, together with a brief description of its location, so that it may be found more easily. Should a cross stand on private land, this has also been indicated, and it needs to be stressed that permission must be sought from the appropriate land-owner before any attempt is made to visit the cross concerned.

The classification of each cross is given with regard to its present-day location, rather than its origin (where different), so as to simplify matters and, hopefully, avoid confusion. For example, the cross in Mary Tavy was originally the village cross, but in 1880 the local churchyard was extended around it and so, in this book, it has been classified as a churchyard cross.

Most of the crosses included in the main section of the book have been measured in the manner indicated by the accompanying diagram. When no measurements are shown for a particular cross, however, this is for one reason only – lack of access. Some are physically out of reach, while the 'vital statistics' of others could only be attained by a totally inappropriate act of mountaineering!

Finally, it should be borne in mind that the few brief comments made about each cross are not intended to represent a complete account of everything that is known about it, as this is considered to be well outside the scope of this book.

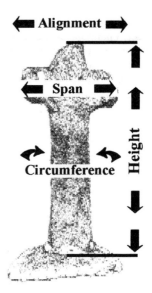

INTRODUCTION

Imagine a warm autumn day, the sun hazy and the visibility good. Well, it was on such a day that I once set out on a walk from Combestone Tor to Fox Tor. At the time I had only just begun to explore Dartmoor and I was soon made to realise that my 'moor-sense' was sadly lacking: after following the O Brook upstream, the sky changed to a grey pall, the wind rose and, having made the mistake of not regularly checking my map, I quickly became hopelessly lost in thick mist!

In desperation, I decided to head northwards in the hope of finding one of the two crosses indicated on the map as being near the top of Ter Hill, knowing that I could then walk on a compass-bearing that would lead me back to Combestone Tor. This, I eventually succeeded in doing, and I can still vividly recall the huge wave of relief that swept over me on that day when one of those granite crosses loomed, somewhat eerily, out of the mist. I can also recall the immense gratitude that I felt to those ancient travellers who had erected that waymarker and how it not only made me see the purpose of the various Dartmoor crosses, but how it also kindled my interest in them.

As time passed and my range of excursions on Dartmoor increased, so I made a point of seeking out as many of the crosses as possible. Moreover, several soon became quite familiar to me as I would often pass the same cross on my many walks. This, in turn, led me to appreciate that these stone sentinels were not inanimate, static features; they are, in fact, changing shape and colour from day to day. For example, on an overcast day, a granite cross may appear grey and sombre, but on a sunny day the effect of the light reflecting off the lichens and the natural granite, highlighting different features, will change the perspective entirely. Other factors can also have an effect, sometimes dramatically, on the appearance of the crosses. These include erosion, brought about by heat, rain, frost and wind, or even the occasional lightning strike, and maltreatment by animals, who, by using the crosses as rubbing posts, often deposit their natural skin oils on the stone, which adds a greasy tinge to the colour.

There are, of course, a number of different types and sizes of crosses. Most of them, though, are constructed of granite, date from between the late Saxon period to the mid-20th century and may be categorised as follows:-

1. **Wayside Crosses** – these were erected for the purpose of marking the various tracks and to serve as guide-posts, both on the open moorland and elsewhere. It has been suggested that the arms of each cross would point in the direction of the track that it marked, but so many of the crosses have been re-erected it is impossible to validate this theory.

2. **Village Crosses** – usually erected upon the village green, these provided the focal point for various activities such as preaching, collecting manorial dues and proclamations.

3. **Churchyard Crosses** – these were normally erected to act as a symbol of sanctity for the church and its grounds, and also to serve as a preaching point. At the coming of Christianity, many of the churches were built on former pagan sites and it is possible that the crosses replaced original pagan stones.

4. **Boundary Crosses** – these were erected to mark the boundaries of manorial and ecclesiastical land. At one time the removal of, or inter-ference with, such crosses was punishable by death.

5. **Market Crosses** – these were erected in the market-place and provided the focal point for fairs, preaching, proclamations and the collection of various dues.

6. **Memorial Crosses** – these tend to be of later origin and usually carry inscriptions or plaques in memory of various people. Some modern-day memorial crosses can also be found, in miniature form, erected on boulders, or rocks, near the favourite locations of deceased persons.

As can be seen from these various categories, anyone who goes in search of the crosses will be taken on a 'pilgrimage' around Dartmoor and be follow-ing in the footsteps of many ancient wayfarers. Before doing so, however, they should remember that when proposing to visit the crosses on the open moorland it is always advisable to carry a map, compass and waterproofs, and to wear suitable clothing and stout walking boots or wellingtons.

Tim Sandles
March 1997

DARTMOOR'S CROSSES

Addiscott Cross

Location: SX667 933 (330 metres north of Fire Stone Cross, on top of the wall by the junction).
Type: Wayside.
Trackway(s): Possibly the Church Path to South Tawton.
Height: 1.37 metres.
Span: 52 centimetres.
Circumference: 93 centimetres.
Alignment: West – East.
Comment(s): In 1874 the cross was moved and re-erected, and in 1958 moved again to its present site.

Beetor Cross

Location: SX713 842 (At the road junction, about 5 kilometres south-west of Moretonhampstead on the B3212).
Type: Wayside.
Trackway(s): Trans – Dartmoor, Exeter – Cornwall Track.
Height: 1.37 metres.
Span: 40 centimetres.
Circumference: 1.15 metres.
Alignment: North-West – South-East.
Comment(s): The cross had been removed at some time prior to the beginning of the 19th century and, in 1857, was in use as a gatepost. It was restored to its present position in 1899 by the Reverend W.H. Thornton.
A legend relates how the cross was erected to commemorate a battle between the Saxons and native Britains. It is also rumoured that a gibbet was erected nearby and a villain hanged in chains from it; apparently he was the last criminal in the locality to be punished in this manner. Horse riders passing this spot have had their reins grabbed by a grizzly spectoral hand.
The site of the cross is known as The Watching Place.

Addiscott Cross

Beetor Cross

Bennet's Cross

Location: SX680 817 (Beside the B3212, near the Warren House Inn).
Type: Wayside.
Trackway(s): Trans – Dartmoor, Exeter – Cornwall Track.
Height: 1.73 metres.
Span: 56 centimetres.
Circumference: 1.24 metres.
Alignment: North – South.
Comment(s): In 1985 the cross was damaged by lightning, possibly the reason why part of the inscription has been lost. It serves as a boundary marker for the parishes of Chagford and North Bovey, and is inscribed with 'WB', which represents Warren Bounds.

Blackaton Bridge Cross

Location: SX678 890 (West of Blackaton Bridge on the northern side of the road opposite the entrance to Blackaton House. It stands on top of the wall).
Type: Wayside.
Trackway(s): None.
Height: 53 centimetres.
Span: 51 centimetres.
Circumference: 1.27 metres.
Alignment: West – East.
Comment(s): During the 1950s the cross was discovered built into the wall upon which it is now erected. There is an incised cross (25 centimetres high and with a span of 26 centimetres) encompassed by a circle on the southern face, and another (20 centimetres high and with a span of 17 centimetres) on the northern face.

It is possible that this cross was one of many affected either by the shaft being removed to serve another purpose, such as a gatepost, or by the Puritan ordinance of 1645; this decreed that all crosses in, or upon, churches and in any open space had to be removed, and resulted in many being broken or even destroyed.

Blackaton Bridge Cross

Bennet's Cross

Blackaton Cross

Location: SX571 631 (Near the end of the old road in the clayworks and about 3 kilometres south-east of Cadover Bridge).
Type: Wayside.
Trackway(s): Plympton – Tavistock Monastic Way.
Height: 1.87 metres.
Span: 64 centimetres.
Circumference: 1.01 metres.
Alignment: North-West – South-East.
Comment(s): The head and arms are mounted on a shaft of later date, which shows signs of possibly having been used as a gatepost due to the presence of a hanger hole on its south-eastern side.
The cross is also known as Roman's Cross, and there is a story that St. Paul once preached here.

The Bovey Stone

Location: SX814 788 (Built into the wall of Cross Cottage on the old Bovey Tracey to Moretonhampstead road, opposite Furzeleigh Lane, which leads to the hospital).
Type: Wayside.
Trackway(s): None.
Height: 25 centimetres (of incised cross).
Span: 17 centimetres (of incised cross).
Circumference: Not applicable.
Alignment: North-West – South-East.
Comment(s): The socket-stone, together with the lower portion of a shaft with a small incised cross on its face, was moved to its present location in 1815 so as to allow for the road to be widened.
Up until the latter part of the 19th century, when, with the advent of the Municipal Corporation Act, the ancient borough of Bovey Tracey came to an end, a time-honoured event known as 'Mayor's Day' took place on the first Monday preceding May the 3rd. This not only featured the beating of the bounds on horseback, but also a tradition whereby the mayor and his party would ride three times around the cross. He would then strike it with a staff to proclaim his authority, after which all the new young freeholders were required to kiss the stone, pledging themselves to uphold the chartered rights and privileges of their Borough.

The Bovey Stone

Blackaton Cross

13

Bovey Tracey – Cross at

Location: SX817 785 (Built into the War Memorial, adjacent to the Town Hall).
Type: Village.
Trackway(s): None.
Height: Unattainable.
Span: Unattainable.
Circumference: Unattainable.
Alignment: North-East – South-West.
Comment(s): The cross is the ancient Market Cross and now serves as the town's War Memorial.
It was moved to its present location in 1865 so that the then new Town Hall could be built, and was adorned with a new head provided by the then vicar of Bovey, the Hon. Canon Courtenay.

Bovey Tracey Church Cross

Location: SX820 785 (In the churchyard bordering the road).
Type: Churchyard.
Trackway(s): None.
Height: 1.85 metres.
Span: 72 centimetres.
Circumference: 1.00 metre.
Alignment: North-West – South-East.
Comment(s): The cross was restored during the early part of the 19th century after the then Lord Courtenay (later Earl of Devon) had discovered the lower portion of the shaft and one of its arms being used as a step near the gate to the churchyard.
However, after having been re-erected near the church on at least two subsequent occasions following acts of vandalism, the cross was removed to Powderham Castle by Lord Courtenay and set up on a pedestal. There it remained until 1849, but when the Hon. Canon Courtenay became vicar of Bovey it was agreed that the cross should be brought back to its rightful home; it was then re-erected at its present location in the churchyard.

Bovey Tracey
Cross at

Bovey Tracey
Church Cross

Buckfast Abbey (1) – Cross at

Location: SX741 674 (Near the entrance to the Abbey and to the west of the other cross mentioned below).
Type: Churchyard.
Trackway(s): None.
Height: 79 centimetres.
Span: 40 centimetres.
Circumference: 70.5 centimetres.
Alignment: West – East.
Comment(s): For some years, up until the 1930s, the cross had been lying buried in the garden of The Old Smithy at Moorshop, 3 kilometres east of Tavistock; it had probably once served as a waymarker.

Initially, after the cross had been found, the intention had been to re-erect it on the nearby roadside, but with the onset of World War II it was presented to the Abbot of Buckfast for safekeeping.

Buckfast Abbey (2) – Cross at

Location: SX741 674 (In the centre of the flower bed near the entrance to the Abbey).
Type: Churchyard.
Trackway(s): None.
Height: 98 centimetres.
Span: 57 centimetres.
Circumference: 1.04 metres.
Alignment: North – South.
Comment(s): The cross, whose origins are unknown, was discovered in the early 1940s at the entrance to Great Palston Farm on the eastern outskirts of South Brent. Although it was broken into two parts, the head having come away from the shaft, these were subsequently rejoined and the cross re-erected at Buckfast Abbey in the interests of preservation.

On each face is a cross outlined by incised lines.

Buckfast Abbey (1)
– Cross at

Buckfast Abbey (2)
– Cross at

17

Buckfastleigh Church – Cross at

Location: SX742 665 (In the churchyard, to the north-east of the church next to a grave of the Furneaux family).
Type: Churchyard.
Trackway(s): None.
Height: 1.08 metres.
Span: 46 centimetres.
Circumference: 61 centimetres.
Alignment: North – South.
Comment(s): Possibly originating as a moorland waymarker, this cross was acquired by the 19th century local historian R. J. King whilst living at nearby Bigadon House. It appears that his intentions were to set it up on Dartmoor, but that never happened. Instead, after the property had come into the ownership of Lt. General Sir J. H. Littler, Lady Littler found the cross and had it removed to its present location to serve as a memorial to a member of the family.

The head of the cross has, at some time, been re-united with the shaft, and a nearby inscription reads: 'Sacred to the memory of Robert Thomas Ryan Littler who died at Bigadon the 6th day of April 1859 aged 51 years'.

Buckland Manor – Cross at

Location: SX721 730 (Halfway along the wall of Buckland Manor and about 45 metres above the gated manor entrance, on the left-hand side when ascending the hill).
Type: Wayside.
Trackway(s): None.
Height: 1.07 metres.
Span: 30 centimetres.
Circumference: Not applicable.
Alignment: Not applicable.
Comment(s): The origins of the cross, possibly used as a gatepost at some time, are unknown.

Buckfastleigh Church - Cross at

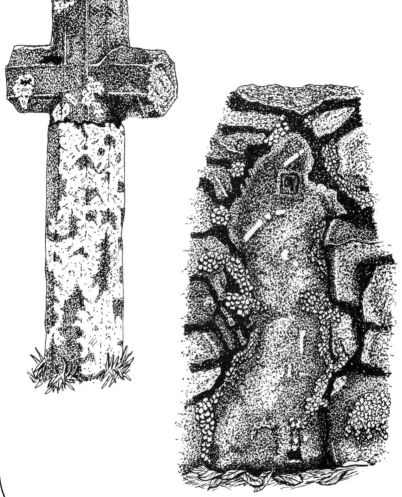

Buckland Manor - Cross at

Buckland-in-the-Moor Church – Cross at

Location: SX720 731 (On top of the churchyard wall, near the south gate).
Type: Churchyard.
Trackway(s): None.
Height: 45 centimetres (shaft) and 58 centimetres (head).
Span: 58 centimetres.
Circumference: Not applicable.
Alignment: Not applicable.
Comment(s): It is possible that the upper portion of the shaft and the arm that now remain were once part of the village cross.

Budleigh Bridge – Cross in

Location: SX762 854 (Built into the parapet of the bridge, on the left-hand side of the A382 road 1.6 kilometres from Moretonhampstead in the direction of Bovey Tracey. Incidentally, according to the current O.S. map the bridge is called One Mill Bridge).
Type: Wayside.
Trackway(s): None.
Height: 49 centimetres.
Span: 51 centimetres.
Circumference: Not applicable.
Alignment: North-West – South-East.
Comment(s): The walls of the bridge were repaired in 1982, at which time Harry Starkey examined the cross and considered that it was no earlier than about 1800. He also speculated that it was a stone-mason's reject.
There is an inscription on the cross that appears to read 1911.

Buckland-in-the-Moor Church - Cross at

Budleigh Bridge - Cross in

Cadover Cross

Location: SX553 647 (On Wigford Down, 200 metres north-west of Cadover Bridge near the wall).
Type: Wayside.
Trackway(s): Plympton – Tavistock Monastic Way.
Height: 2.37 metres.
Span: 77 centimetres.
Circumference: 1.26 metres.
Alignment: North – South.
Comment(s): Only the upper section of the cross and its socket-stone are original, and it is known to have been re-erected at least twice. The first occasion was in 1873 when some soldiers, encamped on Ringmoor Down, found it recumbent and set it up in soil. By 1901, however, the cross was reported as having fallen again, and it was not until 1915 that it was re-erected on its present site by the Reverend H. Hugh Breton, who was fortunate enough to come across the original socket-stone whilst carrying out the work.

The Reverend Breton, who also replaced the shaft, stated that the cross had three incised crosses on its face but, nowadays, these are extremely difficult, if not impossible, to discern.

Canonteign Barton – Cross at

Location: SX838 832 (In the back garden of the house. Please note that this cross stands on private land).
Type: Wayside.
Trackway(s): None.
Height: 2.47 metres.
Span: 65 centimetres.
Circumference: 97 centimetres.
Alignment: North – South.
Comment(s): Very little is known about this cross, except clearly it is not at its original location: it was reportedly removed from the small green at Bridfordmills on the B3193.

Cadover Cross

Canonteign Barton
– Cross at

Chagford Church – Cross at

Location: SX701 875 (North of church, built into war memorial).
Type: Churchyard.
Trackway(s): None.
Height: Unattainable.
Span: Unattainable.
Circumference: Unattainable.
Alignment: North – South.
Comment(s): The head and arms, which were removed from a wall at Holy Street sometime prior to 1928, are the remains of a very old cross that once stood near the market-place. There is an incised cross on its face.

Challabrook Farm – Cross by

Location: SX809 778 (By the footpath from Bovey Tracey leading to Challabrook Farm).
Type: Wayside.
Trackway(s): None.
Height: 1.7 metres.
Span: 48 centimetres.
Circumference: 1.37 metres.
Alignment: South-West – North-East
Comment(s): The cross, which has served as a gatepost at some time, was restored by a local historian called A. J. Wyatt in 1923. It has a plaque that reads 'This old cross once marked the grave of a Royalist officer who fell near here in 1645 when Cromwell's troops defeated the Royalists. A. J. W. 1923.' There is also an incised cross (14 centimetres high and with a span of 12 centimetres) on the south-eastern face.
Sometimes the cross is referred to as Langstone Cross, Langstone possibly being the name of the Royalist officer mentioned on the plaque.

Challabrook Farm - Cross by

Chagford Church - Cross at

Charles Wood – Cross in

Location: SX742 954 (In Charles Wood, above Fingle Bridge and on the left-hand side when ascending the main track to Cranbrook Castle. It is at the point where the main track is intersected by a barriered track).
Type: Wayside.
Trackway(s): None.
Height: 38 centimetres (of incised cross).
Span: 26 centimetres (of incised cross).
Circumference: Not applicable.
Alignment: North-East – South-West.
Comment(s): An old stone pillar with an incised cross that possibly replaced a waymarker of even earlier date: the incised cross can be seen on the north-western face. There is also an O.S. benchmark on the south-western face.

Cheriton Cross

Location: SX773 930 (At a road junction in the village).
Type: Village.
Trackway(s): None.
Height: 81.5 centimetres.
Span: 64 centimetres.
Circumference: 83.5 centimetres.
Alignment: West – East.
Comment(s): Now serving as a War Memorial, and bedded on a large socket-stone, this is a restored cross with a pin through its arms, one of which is a replacement.

Charles Wood
- Cross in

Cheriton Cross

Childe's Tomb – Cross on

Location: SX626 703 (North of Fox Tor in Sand Parks, below the ruins of Fox Tor Farm).
Type: Moorland.
Trackway(s): Buckland – Buckfast Monastic Way.
Height: 1.03 metres.
Span: 51 centimetres.
Circumference: 98 centimetres.
Alignment: North-West – South-East.
Comment(s):   The tomb is supposedly that of Childe the Hunter, who, whilst out hunting, was caught in a snow-storm. In a desperate attempt to stay alive he killed his horse, slit open its belly and crawled inside for shelter.

This was to no avail, but before freezing to death he used the horse's blood to write his Will: 'Whosoever shall find my body and bring it to a burial shall have my lands at Plymstock.'

The legend goes on to say that although the monks of Plympton Priory were first to learn of Childe's fate, it was the monks of Tavistock Abbey who found the body and ultimately claimed the inheritance.

Mount Misery Cross is visible from this location.

Cornwood – Cross at

Location: SX605 597 (In the centre of the village).
Type: Village.
Trackway(s): None.
Height: Unattainable.
Span: Unattainable.
Circumference: Unattainable.
Alignment: South-West – North-East.
Comment(s):   The cross is a memorial to Frederic Rogers, Baron Blachford, who died in 1902.

Cornwood - Cross at

Childe's Tomb - Cross on

Coxtor Gate – Cross at (Head Only)

Location: SX516 763 (About 2 kilometres north of Moorshop, past Headlands Farm on the right-hand verge just after a bend).
Type: Wayside.
Trackway(s): None.
Height: 1.11 metres.
Span: 48 centimetres.
Circumference: 93.5 centimetres.
Alignment: Not applicable.
Comment(s): For many years, up until about 1980, the cross served as a gatepost close to its present location.

Crazywell Cross

Location: SX583 704 (East of Crazywell Pool, below the track).
Type: Moorland.
Trackway(s): Buckfast – Buckland Monastic Way.
Height: 1.38 metres.
Span: 64 centimetres.
Circumference: 84 centimetres.
Alignment: North – South.
Comment(s): The cross was re-erected in 1915 by the Reverend H. Hugh Breton, although only the head and arms are original.
Newleycombe Cross and Hutchinson's Cross are both visible from this location.

Coxtor Gate – Cross at (Head Only)

Crazywell Cross

Cross Gate – Cross at

Location: SX562 695 (At the first road junction north of Burrator Reservoir, near the Devonport Leat).
Type: Wayside.
Trackway(s): Buckfast – Buckland Monastic Way.
Height: 1.86 metres.
Span: 66 centimetres.
Circumference: 73 centimetres.
Alignment: North – South.
Comment(s): The cross could possibly be that reported as having been re-erected by the Reverend H. Hugh Breton in 1915. Another possibility is that it could be the old Lether Tor Cross mentioned in a document dated c1750. In either event, it has been restored with the original head fixed on a shaft of later date.

Cross Park – Cross in

Location: SX777 825 (On the right-hand side of the road, when approaching Higher Combe from the direction of Lustleigh. Please note that this cross stands on private land).
Type: Wayside.
Trackway(s): None.
Height: 72 centimetres.
Span: 64 centimetres.
Circumference: 1.17 metres.
Alignment: North North-West – South South-East.
Comment(s): The cross was mounted on a boulder in 1860 and is named after the field in which it stands.

Cross Gate
– Cross at

Cross Park – Cross in

Drywell Cross

Location: SX701 753 (On the roadside verge of the crossroads just north of Jordan).
Type: Wayside.
Trackway(s): None.
Height: 1.32 metres.
Span: 65 centimetres.
Circumference: 80 centimetres.
Alignment: North North-West – South South-East.
Comment(s): The Dartmoor Preservation Association restored the cross in 1967 by mounting the original head (this had, at some time, been built into a nearby wall) upon a replacement shaft.
It has a rectangular socket cut into its face, possibly to house an icon.

Dunnabridge – Cross near

Location: SX639 738 (Near the ford on the West Dart River. Please note that this cross stands on private land).
Type: Moorland.
Trackway(s): None.
Height: 1.21 metres.
Span: 43 centimetres.
Circumference: 90 centimetres.
Alignment: North North-West – South South-East.
Comment(s): The cross was erected during the winter of 1928/29 in memory of Christopher Holman Richards, who had drowned in the River Dart on 18th August 1928.

Drywell Cross

Dunnabridge
– Cross near

Dunsford Church – Cross at (Head Only)

Location: SX813 892 (By the steps of the churchyard).
Type: Churchyard.
Trackway(s): None.
Height: 46 centimetres.
Span: 40 centimetres.
Circumference: 78.5 centimetres.
Alignment: North – South.
Comment(s): The remains of what was possibly the cross that once stood at the nearby St. Thomas's crossroads were found in the village street serving as a wheel-stop prior to being re-erected.

Elsford Farm – Cross at

Location: SX792 829 (Opposite the lane leading to Lower Elsford Farm).
Type: Wayside.
Trackway(s): Possibly a church track.
Height: 48 centimetres.
Span: 78 centimetres.
Circumference: Unattainable.
Alignment: Not applicable.
Comment(s): The cross was re-discovered in its present site during the early 1980s after having become buried by roadside debris.

Dunsford Church - Cross at (Head Only)

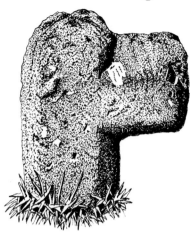

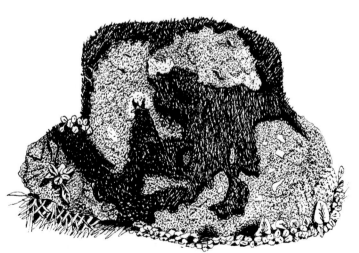

Elsford Farm - Cross at

Fitz's Well – Cross at

Location: SX592 938 (Beside the right-hand side of the road leading to the Okehampton Military Training Camp).
Type: Wayside.
Trackway(s): None.
Height: 84 centimetres.
Span: 49 centimetres.
Circumference: 1.08 metres.
Alignment: North-East – South-West.
Comment(s): The cross may have come from St. Michael's Chapel at nearby Halstock during the period that Sir John Fitz was owner of Okehampton Park, and has an incised cross between the arms. It was supposedly erected by a couple who were 'pixie-led' and became lost on the moor. Having stumbled across a nearby well, they both drank the water and the spell was broken. The cross was the means by which they could express their eternal gratitude.

Gidleigh Church – Cross at

Location: SX670 884 (In the churchyard serving as a marker for a member of the Sampson family).
Type: Churchyard.
Trackway(s): None.
Height: 1.38 metres.
Span: 54 centimetres.
Circumference: 85.5 centimetres.
Alignment: North – South.
Comment(s): The cross was found serving as a fence-post at nearby Greenaway Farm at around 1930 and re-erected, on a new base provided by the Dartmoor Preservation Association, close to the farm entrance. Some years later it was repossessed by the farmer's family and used for the purpose that it now serves.

Fitz's Well
- Cross at

Gidleigh Church
- Cross at

Goldsmith's Cross

Goldsmith's Cross

Location: SX616 701 (East of Whealam Bottom, on the southern edge of Fox Tor Mire).
Type: Moorland.
Trackway(s): Buckfast – Buckland Monastic Way.
Height: 94 centimetres.
Span: 56 centimetres.
Circumference: 1.02 metres.
Alignment: North-East – South-East.
Comment(s): In 1903 the cross was discovered by Lt. Malcolm Goldsmith R.N. (after whom it is named) and re-erected after the head and shaft, found lying and broken on the ground, had been cemented together. The head is now secured to the shaft by an iron clamp.

Gulwell/St. Gudula's Cross

Location: SX753 693 (By the junction of West Street and the Old Totnes Road in Ashburton).
Type: Village.
Trackway(s): None.
Height: 2.21 metres.
Span: 91 centimetres.
Circumference: 51 centimetres.
Alignment: North-East – South-West.
Comment(s): This ancient cross, of which only the upper portion of the shaft, head and arms are original, was restored in 1933 and subsequently re-erected at its present location. Immediately prior to this, the cross had been in two parts at nearby Gulwell Farm. Here the remains of the shaft had been utilised as the top of a small mounting block, and the head and arms used to support a cider vat.

It is believed that the cross, thought to date back to the 14th century, originally stood by an old well in the near vicinity, called Gulwell. There is also a legend that the water from this well had a beneficial effect on those with ailing eye-sight and that, in consequence, the cross was erected and named after Gudula, a Flemish saint and patron of blind people.

Gulwell/St. Gudula's Cross

Hameldown Cross

Location: SX704 801 (About 500 metres south south-east of Hameldown Tor).
Type: Wayside.
Trackway(s): Possibly the Church Path to Widecombe.
Height: 1.34 metres.
Span: 66 centimetres.
Circumference: 1.28 metres.
Alignment: North-South.
Comment(s): The cross carries the inscription HC (Hameldown Cross) – DS (Duke of Somerset) – 1854 and serves as a boundary marker for the Manor of Natsworthy.

Harford Church – Cross at

Location: SX638 594 (Inside the gate of the churchyard).
Type: Churchyard.
Trackway(s): None.
Height: 1.36 metres.
Span: 38 centimetres.
Circumference: 1.03 metres.
Alignment: North – South.
Comment(s): In the 1930s the cross was found being used as a gatepost near its present location and at one time was possibly sited on the moor to serve as a marker for the Plympton to Buckfast Monastic Way.

Hameldown Cross

Harford Church
- Cross at

Hawson Cross

Location: SX710 682 (About 3 kilometres north-west of Buckfast, at the crossroads beside an old oak tree (Stumpy Oak).
Type: Wayside.
Trackway(s): Probably Buckfast – Buckland Monastic Way.
Height: 2.21 metres.
Span: 82 centimetres.
Circumference: 1.155 metres.
Alignment: West – East.
Comment(s): Up until around the end of the 19th century the upper portion of the cross had been sited in a nearby hedge. It was then moved and re-erected at its present location.
In 1952 the cross was restored by the Dartmoor Preservation Association and a new shaft added.

Hele Cross

Location: SX721 841 (At the crossroads near Hele Farm).
Type: Wayside.
Trackway(s): None.
Height: 1.75 metres.
Span: 63 centimetres.
Circumference: 94.5 centimetres.
Alignment: North – South.
Comment(s): According to tradition, the cross originated from a small, nearby chapel. It was said that Tavistock-bound pilgrims would gather and pray around the cross for guidance and deliverance from the perils of the awaiting moor.

Hawson Cross

Hele Cross

Hexworthy Cross

Hexworthy Cross

Location: SX656 726 (On the small green adjacent to the Forest Inn).
Type: Village.
Trackway(s): None.
Height: 2.32 metres.
Span: 76 centimetres.
Circumference: 1.005 metres.
Alignment: North – South.
Comment(s): Erected in 1897 to commemorate Queen Victoria's Diamond Jubilee, the cross has inscribed on its western face a crown and VR — 1837 – 1897, plus the following: Also to the glory of God – in commemoration of the – 60 years of – Queen Victoria's reign.
Although this is a relatively modern cross, it is the only example of a celtic cross to be found on Dartmoor, apart from in grave-yards.

Hobajohn's Cross

Location: SX655 605 (Approximately 2 kilometres south of Three Barrows).
Type: Moorland.
Trackway(s): None.
Height: 19 centimetres (of incised cross).
Span: 14 centimetres (of incised cross).
Circumference: Not applicable.
Alignment: North-West – South-East.
Comment(s): A granite pillar with an incised cross that lies at the boundary of the parishes of Ugborough and Harford.

Hobajohn's Cross

Holne Church – Cross at

Location: SX706 695 (At the head of Reverend Gill's grave, near the war memorial and a large split yew tree).
Type: Churchyard.
Trackway(s): None.
Height: 1.29 metres.
Span: 69 centimetres.
Circumference: 79.5 centimetres.
Alignment: North – South.
Comment(s): The cross, which may once have stood at Play Cross (SX705 693), has served as a gatepost, three holes on its south-western face testifying to this fact. At some time prior to 1870, however, it was restored with new arms, furnished with a pedestal and erected in the churchyard at the behest of a local resident.
It is possible that the original socket-stone is incorporated into the nearby War Memorial.

Horn's Cross

Location: SX669 711 (On Holne Moor, about 800 metres south of Combestone Tor).
Type: Moorland.
Trackway(s): Buckfast – Buckland Monastic Way.
Height: 1.95 metres.
Span: 57 centimetres.
Circumference: 1.31 metres.
Alignment: North-East – South-West.
Comment(s): The cross is also known as 'Stacombe's Telling-place', a name derived from the practice of a local farmer who would gather and count his stock here. This was referred to as 'telling', hence telling-place.
The cross has been restored by means of securing its rather mutilated head to a comparatively modern shaft using an iron clamp.
Skir Ford Cross, Horse Ford Cross, Ter Hill Cross (East) and Ter Hill Cross (West) are all visible from this location.

Holne Church
~ Cross at

Horn's Cross

Horrabridge – Cross at

Location: SX513 699 (Built into the northern parapet of the bridge that spans the River Walkham at Horrabridge).
Type: Village.
Trackway(s): None.
Height: 59 centimetres (of incised cross).
Span: 27 centimetres (of incised cross).
Circumference: Unattainable.
Alignment: North-East – South-West.
Comment(s): A granite stone with an incised cross.

Horse Ford Cross

Location: SX660 713 (By the old Hexworthy Mine track above the O Brook).
Type: Moorland.
Trackway(s): Buckfast – Buckland Monastic Way.
Height: 1.06 metres.
Span: 70 centimetres.
Circumference: 96.5 centimetres.
Alignment: North-West – South-East.
Comment(s): The cross was restored at the behest of William Crossing shortly after having been re-discovered by a labourer from Hexworthy in 1884. It was done by securing the head of the cross to the remains of its shaft, which was lying on the ground nearby.
In 1972 the cross was restored again after having been found recumbent, probably as a result of animals rubbing against it. On this occasion the work was carried out by two officials of the Dartmoor National Park Authority, who used an iron bracket to secure the two sections of the cross.
Horn's Cross is visible from this location.

Horrabridge – Cross at

Horse Ford Cross

Horsepit Cross

Location: SX743 847 (At Bovey Cross, about 1 kilometre from North Bovey).
Type: Wayside.
Trackway(s): None.
Height: 99 centimetres.
Span: 56 centimetres.
Circumference: 58 centimetres.
Alignment: North North-East – South South-East.
Comment(s): The cross is inscribed with a possible O.S. benchmark and the letters O (Okehampton), N (Newton Abbot), M (Moretonhampstead) and B (Bovey).

Huckworthy Common – Cross on

Location: SX530 711 (At the road junction, near a cattle grid and on a mound of earth).
Type: Moorland.
Trackway(s): Plympton – Tavistock Monastic Way.
Height: 1.96 metres.
Span: 54 centimetres.
Circumference: 1.155 metres.
Alignment: North – South.
Comment(s): There is an O.S. benchmark on the southern face of the shaft.

Horsepit Cross

Huckworthy Common
- Cross on

Huntingdon Cross

Location: SX664 661 (Above the confluence of The Avon and The Wester Wella Brook).
Type: Moorland.
Trackway(s): Jobbers' Road (Abbots' Way).
Height: 1.38 metres.
Span: 56 centimetres.
Circumference: 96 centimetres.
Alignment: North – South.
Comment(s): The original purpose of this ancient cross was almost certainly to serve as a marker along the Jobbers' Road from Sheepstor to Buckfastleigh but, in 1557, it was brought into use to mark the boundary of Brent Moor.

Hutchinson's Cross

Location: SX599 699 (By the Devonport Leat, about 800 metres west of Nun's Cross Farm).
Type: Moorland.
Trackway(s): Buckfast – Buckland Monastic Way.
Height: 1.43 metres.
Span: 61 centimetres.
Circumference: 86 centimetres.
Alignment: North North-East – South South-West.
Comment(s): The cross, inscribed with 'S.L.H. 1887–1966', was erected in 1968 by Lt. Commander B. Hutchinson R.N. as a memorial to his mother. It is set in a socket cut in a large boulder, which was used for a cross of much earlier date that disappeared. Newleycombe Cross and Crazywell Cross are both clearly visible from this location.

Huntingdon Cross

Hutchinson's Cross

Keble Martin's Cross

Location: SX666 666 (On the left-hand bank of the Wester Wella Brook, about 450 metres above its confluence with The Avon).
Type: Moorland.
Trackway(s): None.
Height: 15.5 centimetres (of incised cross).
Span: 14 centimetres (of incised cross).
Circumference: Not applicable.
Alignment: North-West – South-East.
Comment(s): Keble Martin's Chapel was constructed out of a natural hollow during the early part of the 20th century by a group of young men led by the Reverend Keble Martin, who used to visit the area and camp here.

At the northern end of the 'hollow', the floor was raised by means of a slab and a cross incised on the south-western face of a small, erect rock by the clergyman's brother, Arthur, so as to form an altar for morning worship.

The site, sometimes called Mattins Corner, has also been used for a child's baptism and, much more recently, for a wedding.

Leeper (Liapa) Cross

Location: SX702 833 (Just off the B3212, about 1.6 kilometres from Beetor Cross, by a gate on the bank of the wall).
Type: Wayside.
Trackway(s): Mariners' Way and Trans – Dartmoor, Exeter – Cornwall Track.
Height: 1.07 metres.
Span: 59 centimetres.
Circumference: 1.24 metres.
Alignment: North-East – South-West.
Comment(s): The cross was found built into a wall at Liapa (now Moor Gate) Farm, but shortly after the beginning of the 20th century it was taken away to the Manor House, North Bovey, at the behest of Viscount Hambledon, then Lord of the Manor.

In 1937, however, by which time the Manor had been sold, the cross was re-erected at its present location.

There is a raised cross on each face.

Keble Martin's Cross

Leigh Bridge
- Cross by

Leeper (Liapa) Cross

Leigh Bridge – Cross by

Location: SX683 876 (High up on top of a bank on the left-hand side of the road approaching the bridge, on a large boulder amongst the trees).
Type: Wayside.
Trackway(s): None.
Height: 1.22 metres.
Span: 38 centimetres.
Circumference: 80 centimetres.
Alignment: West – East.
Comment(s): The head of the cross, which was removed from nearby Teigncombe shortly after the beginning of the 20th century, has been mounted on a shaft of later date.

Linscott Cross

Location: SX741 872 (On the right-hand side of the road, 183 metres past Howton farm).
Type: Wayside.
Trackway(s): None.
Height: 1.52 metres.
Span: 55 centimetres.
Circumference: 1.235 metres.
Alignment: North-West – South-East.
Comment(s): This badly mutilated cross was discovered at the end of the 19th century serving as a gatepost, evidence of which is provided by the three slots and hinge hole apparent on the north-eastern side and the metal pin on the north-western side.

In c1902 it was erected at its present location, which was considered to be the nearest suitable spot to that where it had been found.

There is also an incised cross (25 centimetres high and with a span of 17 centimetres) on the south-western face.

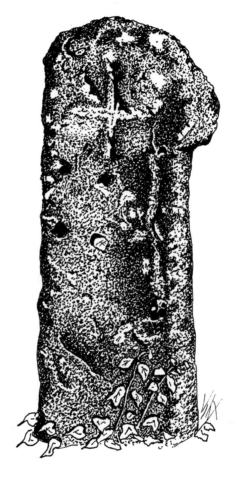

Linscott Cross

Lower Dunstone – Cross at

Location: SX716 758 (About 1 kilometre from Widecombe-in-the-Moor, on the small green adjacent to the farm).
Type: Wayside.
Trackway(s): None.
Height: 93 centimetres.
Span: 58 centimetres.
Circumference: 1.07 metres.
Alignment: North-East – South-West.
Comment(s): Although the cross originally stood at its present location, it was removed by a former vicar of Widecombe at some time between the years 1815 and 1860, and fixed at the end of a low wall in the vicarage garden for preservation.
A plaque attached to the plinth on which the cross now stands tells the rest of the story: Dunstone Cross back in its – original site after 100 years – in the vicarage garden – restored by – Miss M. Hamlyn. Dunstone Manor – 1980.

(The adjacent granite boulder (after which the hamlet may have been named, and which has been referred to as 'The Rent Stone') marks the spot where, in former times, the manor courts were held. It is said that the chief rents were deposited in a hollow on this stone and that when the Black Death was prevalent the hollow was filled with vinegar so as to disinfect the coins)

Lower Dunstone – Cross at

Lustleigh – Cross at

Location: SX785 812 (On the village green at Lustleigh, opposite the church).
Type: Village.
Trackway(s): None.
Height: Unattainable.
Span: Unattainable.
Circumference: Unattainable.
Alignment: North – South.
Comment(s): The cross was erected in memory of the Rector of Lustleigh Parish from 1888-1904. An inscription on the pedestal reads: In pious memory of Harry Tudor, Rector of this Parish. There is also a tiny incised cross between the first and last words of the inscription.

Manaton Church – Cross at

Location: SX749 813 (Just beyond the south door of the church).
Type: Churchyard.
Trackway(s): None.
Height: 1.81 metres.
Span: 27 centimetres.
Circumference: 1.18 metres.
Alignment: North – South.
Comment(s): The original cross disappeared in 1841 and has never been found. At the time it was rumoured that the then newly-appointed Rector of Manaton parish had removed it as a means of putting an end to a local custom of which he disapproved and one that entailed the coffin of a deceased person being carried, three times, around the cross prior to being taken into the church.

The present-day cross, which has a small incised cross (17.5 centimetres high and with a span of 16 centimetres) on its western face and another (20 centimetres high and with a span of 15 centimetres) on its eastern face, was discovered built into a nearby wall in 1908 by a local workman. Originally, it was believed that this was the cross which had gone missing, and so it was subsequently slotted into the empty socket-stone in the churchyard. However, this cannot be the case for the cross does not properly fit into the socket-stone, which bears testimony to the work of a skilled mason.

Lustleigh – Cross at

Marchant's Cross

Location: SX546 668 (Just south of Marchant's Bridge, opposite a farm).
Type: Wayside.
Trackway(s): Plympton – Tavistock Monastic Way and Jobbers' Road (Abbots' Way).
Height: 2.37 metres.
Span: 69 centimetres.
Circumference: 1.115 metres.
Alignment: North North-East – South South-West.
Comment(s): This is the only cross standing on the supposed western arm of the Abbots' Way. There is an incised cross (65 centimetres high and with a span of 33 centimetres) on its western face and a similar one (69 centimetres high and with a span of 34 centimetres) on its eastern face.
The cross is also supposed to mark the grave of a suicide, and travellers setting out over the moor were once said to kneel in front of it to pray for protection on their journey.

Mary Tavy Church – Cross at (Head Only)

Location: SX509 787 (Inside the churchyard, beneath the 'village' cross).
Type: Churchyard.
Trackway(s): None.
Height: 36 centimetres.
Span: 29 centimetres.
Circumference: 62 centimetres.
Alignment: Not applicable.
Comment(s): This is the original head of the 'village' cross and was found in the late 1930s.

Mary Tavy
Church –
Cross at
(Head Only)

Marchant's
Cross

Manaton Church – Cross at

Mary Tavy Church – Cross at

Location: SX509 787 (Inside the churchyard).
Type: Churchyard.
Trackway(s): None.
Height: 1.84 metres.
Span: 45 centimetres.
Circumference: 67.5 centimetres.
Alignment: West – East.
Comment(s): Although classed as a churchyard cross since 1880, when the churchyard was extended and enclosed it, this cross is actually the village cross.
It has a replacement head, and flowers are carved in relief on the sides.

The Maximajor Stone

Location: SX771 878 (On Mardon Down, opposite spot height 319 on the side of the road).
Type: Wayside.
Trackway(s): None.
Height: 1.69 metres.
Span: Not applicable.
Circumference: 1.195 metres.
Alignment: Not applicable.
Comment(s): Although also referred to as the Headless Cross, the Maximajor Stone has served no known purpose and may well have been a prehistoric menhir.
The present-day stone, however, is a replica that was erected by the Dartmoor National Park Authority in 1992. This came about as the result of a mindless act of vandalism some two years earlier when a car was driven into the original stone and set alight; the resultant heat caused the stone to break into three pieces rendering it irreparable.

The Maximajor Stone

Mary Tavy Church – Cross at

Meavy Cross

Location: SX540 672 (On the village green, near The Meavy Oak).
Type: Village.
Trackway(s): None.
Height: Unattainable.
Span: Unattainable.
Circumference: Unattainable.
Alignment: North-West – South-East.
Comment(s): After having gone missing for more than 100 years, the shaft of the cross was discovered serving as a gatepost in a nearby field during the latter part of the 19th century by the then vicar of Meavy.

Complete restoration of the cross, using a new head, followed in 1895, and it was subsequently re-erected at its present (and original) location, where the base and pedestal had remained undisturbed.

Moon's Cross

Location: SX652 941 (At the road junction about 300 metres south of South Tawton).
Type: Wayside.
Trackway(s): None.
Height: 80 centimetres.
Span: Not applicable.
Circumference: 1.29 metres.
Alignment: Not applicable.
Comment(s): Little appears to be known about the cross or when it was broken.

Moon's Cross

Meavy Cross

Moretonhampstead – Cross at (Head Only)

Location: SX755 860 (Near the 'Cross Tree', by the south gate of the church).
Type: Village.
Trackway(s): None.
Height: 57 centimetres.
Span: 74 centimetres.
Circumference: 1.175 metres.
Alignment: North North-East – South South-West.
Comment(s): The cross has a 'T'-shaped recess on one face and another, almost rectangular, recess on its other face, added to which the top of the head has a small cavity. These would possibly have housed icons.

Mount Misery Cross

Location: SX636 706 (In the eastern corner of Fox Tor Newtake).
Type: Moorland.
Trackway(s): Buckfast – Buckland Monastic Way.
Height: 1.66 metres.
Span: 73 centimetres.
Circumference: 94.5 centimetres.
Alignment: North – South.
Comment(s): The cross was re-erected in 1885 by fixing the shaft in its socket with cement after it had been found recumbent by William Crossing on at least two occasions over the previous 7 years, probably as a result of animals rubbing against it.
In 1881 Crossing also found the top portion of another cross in the vicinity and considered that this might well have been the original head of the cross on Childe's Tomb, which can clearly be seen just over a kilometre away from this location.

Moretonhampstead – Cross at (Head Only)

Mount Misery Cross

Newleycombe Cross

Location: SX592 703 (On the south side of the Whiteworks – Lowery Track).
Type: Moorland.
Trackway(s): Buckfast – Buckland Monastic Way.
Height: 1.88 metres.
Span: 58 centimetres.
Circumference: 75 centimetres.
Alignment: West – East.
Comment(s): The cross was re-erected in 1915 by the Reverend H. Hugh Breton, although only the head, arms and upper part of the shaft are original. In 1989 the cross also underwent repairs, carried out by the Dartmoor National Park Authority.
Both Crazywell Cross and Hutchinson's Cross can be seen from this location.

North Bovey – Cross at

Location: SX740 839 (On the village green, opposite The Ring O' Bells).
Type: Village.
Trackway(s): None.
Height: 1.24 metres.
Span: 63 centimetres.
Circumference: 66 centimetres.
Alignment: North – South.
Comment(s): For many years, up until 1829, the present-day cross was serving as a footbridge over a stream just below the village. It was then moved to its present site at the behest of a former curate of North Bovey and re-erected, the shaft being secured in the original socket-stone by four small iron clamps.
The original cross was broken during the Civil War and, in 1943, was found to have been built into the parlour wall of a nearby cottage.

North Bovey
- Cross at

Newleycombe Cross

Nun's (Siward's) Cross

Location: SX605 699 (Near Nun's Cross Farm).
Type: Moorland.
Trackway(s): Buckfast to Tavistock Monastic Way and Jobbers' Road (Abbots' Way).
Height: 2.07 metres.
Span: 76 centimetres.
Circumference: 1.46 metres.
Alignment: North – South.
Comment(s): The cross is generally believed to be of the late Saxon period, or early medieval, and was mentioned in the Perambulation of 1240 as being a boundary mark for the Forest of Dartmoor.
Both sides of the cross also carry inscriptions. On the eastern face is the word 'Siwardi', an inscription that was possibly made so that the cross could serve as a boundary mark for the lands granted by Edward the Confessor to Siward, Earl of Northumberland, while on the western face are the words 'BOC LOND'. These are almost certainly a derivation of the name Buckland, meaning book land (or land held by charter), and are believed to be connected with the monks of Buckland Abbey, who came into possession of the Manor of Walkhampton in the late 13th century and for which the cross was already being used as a boundary mark.
According to William Crossing, the shaft of the cross was broken into two parts in 1846 by a couple of youths looking for cattle on the moor, but was soon repaired and re-erected.

Okehampton Church – Cross at

Location: SX582 951 (Near the west gate of the churchyard).
Type: Churchyard.
Trackway(s): None.
Height: 2.07 metres.
Span: 47.5 centimetres.
Circumference: 76 centimetres.
Alignment: North – South.
Comment(s): The cross was found in 1928 serving as a nearby gatepost. It was then restored with a new head and arms and re-erected at its present location. There are O.S. benchmarks on the western, southern and eastern faces.

Nun's (Siward's) Cross

Okehampton Church
- Cross at

Ouldsbroom Cross

Location: SX684 735 (At the road junction, also named Ouldsbroom Cross).
Type: Wayside.
Trackway(s): Possibly the Church Path to Widecombe Church.
Height: 1.57 metres.
Span: 46 centimetres.
Circumference: 1.46 metres.
Alignment: West – East.
Comment(s): The cross was re-erected at its present (and possibly original) location in the early 1950s after having been taken away in c1825 to serve as a gatepost at Town Farm, Leusdon. It was then that the arms had been knocked off!

Oxenham Cross

Location: SX663 944 (About 1 kilometre east of South Tawton, high up on a bank beside a field gate at the crossroads).
Type: Wayside.
Trackway(s): None.
Height: 1.53 metres.
Span: 57 centimetres.
Circumference: 1.105 metres.
Alignment: West – East.
Comment(s): Towards the end of the 19th century, William Crossing discovered the upper part of the cross in a nearby hedge, and shortly afterwards this was placed on the remains of the shaft. Later, in the 1930s, the two sections were cemented together, but then subsequently came apart. As a result, in 1951, the cross was restored and re-erected on its present site under the auspices of the Dartmoor Preservation Association.

There is an incised cross (19 centimetres high and with a span of 20 centimetres) on the northern face.

Oxenham Cross

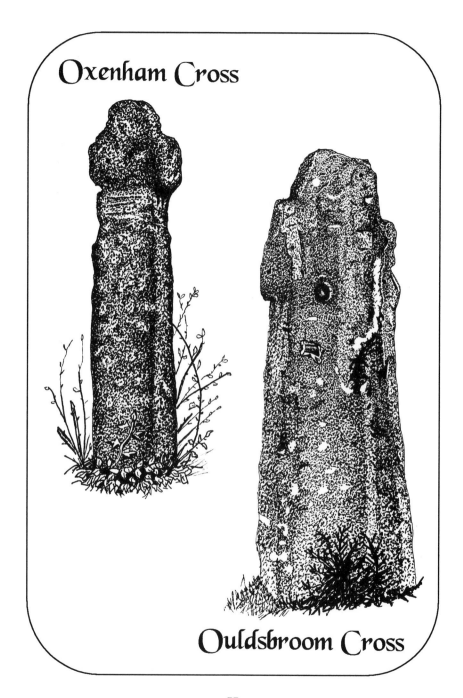

Ouldsbroom Cross

Petre's Cross

Location: SX653 654 (On the cairn at Western Whittabarrow).
Type: Moorland.
Trackway(s): None.
Height: 87 centimetres.
Span: Not applicable.
Circumference: 1.06 metres.
Alignment: Not applicable.
Comment(s): The cross was erected in 1557 to mark the boundary of Brent Moor and is named after Sir William Petre, who was the Lord of the Manor at that time.

Unfortunately, during the mid-19th century the arms of the cross were broken off by some men working on the nearby peat-ties and the shaft used as a lintel for the fireplace in a hut that they constructed from stones taken off the cairn. Not long after, the hut fell into dis-use and, eventually, the shaft of the cross was found amongst the ruins. It was then re-erected to serve, once again, as a boundary mark, and has since been inscribed with an O.S. benchmark.

Pixies' Cross

Location: SX501 737 (On the golf course, 183 metres from the road and in a small quarry on Whitchurch Down).
Type: Wayside.
Trackway(s): Buckfast – Tavistock Monastic Way and Jobbers' Road (Abbots' Way).
Height: 2.24 metres.
Span: 77 centimetres.
Circumference: 1.23 metres.
Alignment: North – South.
Comment(s): It is said that a local Puritan vicar once gave instructions for the cross to be taken away. However, no-one would undertake the job for fear of divine retribution, so the vicar headed out to do the dire deed himself.

Almost as soon as he had set to work, the vicar found himself confronted by a big, black bull, whose intentions were all too obvious. In response, the vicar quickly decided that the only place of refuge was on top of the cross, so this is where he scrambled.

Pixies' Cross

Petre's Cross

The bull was rather determined and ensured that the vicar spent all night perched on the cross. Then, in the early morning mist, a local woman passed by the spot. Mistaking the pair for the devil and his familiar, she immediately fled, panic-stricken, to a nearby village and reported what she had just seen.

This, not unnaturally, aroused the curiosity of the local folk. They made off for the cross and, on their arrival, discovered the truth. The bull was then taken away, but only after the vicar had given his pledge that the cross would remain intact.

Clearly he kept his word as the cross still stands!

Postbridge – Cross at

Location: SX653 793 (In the wall near the gateway of Stannon Lodge and opposite the chapel).
Type: Wayside.
Trackway(s): Possibly Trans – Dartmoor, Exeter – Cornwall Track.
Height: 52 centimetres.
Span: 33 centimetres.
Circumference: Not applicable.
Alignment: Not applicable.
Comment(s): This is possibly the remains of Maggie Cross, which stood close to the nearby lodge gate until disappearing during the latter part of the 19th century.

Princetown Church – Cross at

Location: SX586 737 (The largest cross in the churchyard, to the north-west of the church).
Type: Churchyard.
Trackway(s): None.
Height: Unattainable.
Span: Unattainable.
Circumference: Unattainable.
Alignment: North-West – South-East.
Comment(s): The cross, made in Dartmoor Prison by convict labour, was erected in 1912 as a memorial to all those prisoners who lie in unmarked graves.

Postbridge - Cross at

Princetown Church - Cross at

Ridding Down – Cross on

Location: SX586 612 (Just inside the field gateway above Tinpark Farm).
Type: Wayside.
Trackway(s): None.
Height: 1.67 metres.
Span: 36 centimetres.
Circumference: 1.11 metres.
Alignment: North North-West – South South-East.
Comment(s): The cross was never properly completed and has previously been used as a gatepost as is clearly evident from the two metal hangers and hole on its southern side. Next to it is the arm, or part of the shaft, of another cross, which was possibly the one that had also stood at this same location from 1969 until disappearing in 1978. This, too, had previously served as a gatepost and, for many years, had been situated just inside the entrance of the nearby lane leading to Cholwich Town Farm.

Ringhole Copse – Cross at

Location: SX672 942 (At the road junction, about 2 kilometres east of South Tawton, overlooking the A30).
Type: Wayside.
Trackway(s): Possibly the Church Path to South Tawton.
Height: 1.92 metres.
Span: 57 centimetres.
Circumference: 1.07 centimetres.
Alignment: North – South.
Comment(s): The cross has two incised crosses, one (26 centimetres high and with a span of 21.5 centimetres) on its western face and another with the same dimensions on its eastern face.

Ridding Down - Cross on

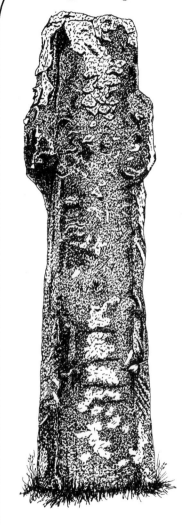

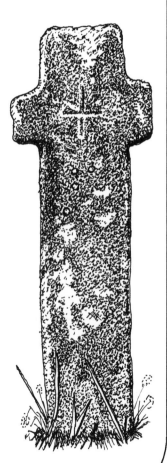

Ringhole Copse - Cross at

Rippon Tor – Cross on

Location: SX747 756 (Near the summit of Rippon Tor, on its north-western side).
Type: Moorland.
Trackway(s): None.
Height: 2.02 metres.
Span: 58 centimetres.
Circumference: Not applicable.
Alignment: Not applicable.
Comment(s): A cross cut in relief on a large block of granite, whose purpose is unknown.

Sampford Spiney – Cross at

Location: SX534 724 (On the village green, near the church).
Type: Village.
Trackway(s): None.
Height: 1.16 metres.
Span: 51 centimetres.
Circumference: 70.5 centimetres.
Alignment: North North-West – South South-East.
Comment(s): The cross formerly stood in a nearby hedge and was moved to its present site in the 19th century by the then Lord of the Manor.

Rippon Tor
- Cross on

Sampford Spiney
- Cross at

Sanduck Cross

Location: SX768 836 (On the roadside near Sanduck Farm).
Type: Wayside.
Trackway(s): None.
Height: 1.24 metres.
Span: 36 centimetres.
Circumference: 88 centimetres.
Alignment: North-East – South-West.
Comment(s): In 1901 Sanduck Farm was burned down and the cross was discovered in the foundations. At some time it has been given a replacement arm.

Shaden Moor – Cross on

Location: SX552 634 (On the roadside between Cadover Bridge and Shaugh Prior).
Type: Wayside.
Trackway(s): Plympton – Tavistock Monastic Way.
Height: 2.1 metres.
Span: 58 centimetres.
Circumference: 1.105 metres.
Alignment: South-West – North-East.
Comment(s): According to William Crossing, the cross (sometimes referred to as Stony Cross) was formerly used as the bottom stone of a nearby stile.
It was re-erected in 1915 by the Reverend H. Hugh Breton, having for many years been propped up against the nearby wall, although only the head, arms and upper part of the shaft are original.

Sanduck Cross

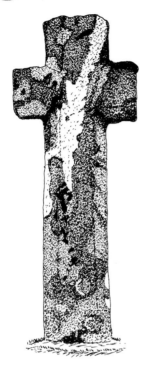

Shaden Moor
- Cross on

Shaugh Prior – Cross at

Location: SX544 630 (In a wall, near the vicarage).
Type: Wayside.
Trackway(s): Plympton – Buckland/Tavistock Monastic Way.
Height: 1.7 metres.
Span: 66 centimetres.
Circumference: 1.03 metres.
Alignment: South South-West – North North-East.
Comment(s): Nothing appears to be known about the origins of the cross, which has had one of its arms repaired at some time.

Sheepstor Church – Cross at

Location: SX560 676 (By the stile at the top of the steps leading from the Playfield, to the south of the church).
Type: Churchyard.
Trackway(s): None.
Height: 1.74 metres.
Span: 63 centimetres.
Circumference: 81 centimetres.
Alignment: North – South.
Comment(s): The cross was, at one time, in use as one of the posts forming a stile at the top of the steps leading from the Playfield, and has since had new arms fitted.

Shaugh Prior
~ Cross at

Sheepstor Church
~ Cross at

Sheepstor – Cross at

Location: SX560 676 (Just outside the churchyard near the lych-gate).
Type: Village.
Trackway(s): None.
Height: 1.62 metres.
Span: 67 centimetres.
Circumference: 1.10 metres.
Alignment: North-West – South-East.
Comment(s): For many years the cross, also known as St. Rumon's Cross at one time, had stood in a field at Burrator and had previously served as a gatepost. In 1910, however, the cross was returned to its rightful place in the middle of the parish, given new arms and re-erected on a large base (built by some of the local inhabitants) as a memorial of the Coronation of King George V; it was dedicated by the Reverend H. Hugh Breton on the afternoon of Coronation Day – June 22nd, 1911 – in order that it could be used as a preaching cross and open-air services held there.
There is an incised cross on each face.

Sherril/Cave-Penney Cross

Location: SX683 738 (On Corndon Down, above the Ouldsbroom – Babeny road).
Type: Moorland.
Trackway(s): None.
Height: 1.305 metres.
Span: 57 centimetres.
Circumference: 74.5 centimetres.
Alignment: North North-West – South South-East.
Comment(s): The cross stands on a boulder known as 'The Belstone Bible' and was erected in memory of a member of the Cave-Penney family from nearby Sherril. An inscription at the base of the cross reads: To the glory of God – and to the dear memory of – Evelyn Anthony Cave-Penney – Lieut. O.V.O. corps of guides – fell in Palestine whilst – gallantly commanding his men – June 8th 1918 aged 19 – look up and lift your heads.

Sherril/Cave-Penney Cross

Sheepstor – Cross at

Shorter Cross

Location: SX713 864 (By the right-hand side of the road, 400 metres past Middlecott Farm).
Type: Wayside.
Trackway(s): None.
Height: 1.65 metres.
Span: Not applicable.
Circumference: 1.25 metres.
Alignment: Not applicable.
Comment(s): In 1873 the cross (possibly one of Devon's earliest crosses dating back to between the 7th and 9th centuries) was taken away to nearby Middlecott Farm and sited under a pump. There it remained until 1900, when it was returned to its original location.

The cross has a cross cut in relief on its south-western face (55 centimetres high and with a span of 28 centimetres), an incised cross (38 centimetres high and with a span of 28 centimetres) on its north-eastern face, and another incised cross (12 centimetres high and with a span of 11 centimetres) on its south-western face.

Skir Ford Cross

Location: SX654 714 (On Down Ridge, north of the Hensroost Mine).
Type: Moorland.
Trackway(s): Buckfast – Buckland Monastic Way.
Height: 1.49 metres.
Span: 70 centimetres.
Circumference: 96 centimetres.
Alignment: North-East – South-West.
Comment(s): The cross was restored in 1885 by William Crossing, who clamped the top portion to the lower part of the shaft, which had previously been missing, and set it on a mound. It has since been cemented into a boulder.

Horns Cross, Ter Hill Cross (East) and Ter Hill Cross (West) are all visible from this location.

Shorter Cross

Skir Ford Cross

Sourton Down – Cross on

Location: SX546 916 (At the entrance to Sourton Down Caravan Park, behind The Prewley Arms).
Type: Wayside.
Trackway(s): None.
Height: 2.10 metres.
Span: 53 centimetres.
Circumference: 1.275 metres.
Alignment: North-East – South-West.
Comment(s): The shaft is thought, originally, to have been an early Christian memorial stone that was later converted into a wayside cross. It has inscribed on it a Chi-rol symbol as well as the words PRINCIPI IVRIVOCI AUDETI, which has been suggested is a personal name and title.

For many years the cross was sited just to the south of the junction of the A386 and the A30, but during the late 1980s it was removed, temporarily, to Okehampton Castle for safekeeping whilst the new A30 was being built.

The cross has inscribed on its north-western face the letter H (Hatherleigh), on its south-eastern face the letter T (Tavistock), on its north-eastern face O (Okehampton) and on its south-western face L (Launceston).

Sourton Green Saxon Cross

Location: SX534 903 (On the village green, opposite The Highwayman Inn).
Type: Village.
Trackway(s): None.
Height: 1.73 metres.
Span: Not applicable.
Circumference: 1.025 metres.
Alignment: Not applicable.
Comment(s): This granite pillar has been identified as a 10th century Saxon memorial stone. It is also known as the 'Oxo' stone for obvious reasons.

A plaque on a nearby boulder reads: This Christian stone – dates to about the 10th century AD – found at East Linnacombe. It was repaired – and erected here by the – Dartmoor National Park – Authority in 1985.

Sourton Down
- Cross on

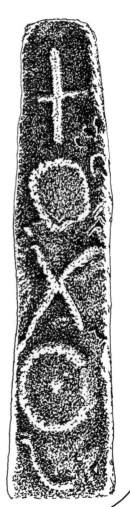

Sourton Green
Saxon Cross

South Harton – Cross at

Location: SX772 822 (In the wall at the entrance to South Harton Farm).
Type: Wayside.
Trackway(s): None.
Height: 1.86 metres.
Span: 57 centimetres.
Circumference: 1.68 metres.
Alignment: North – South.
Comment(s): The cross was re-erected at its present location by a former occupier of the farm during the 19th century. Previously, it had been split down the middle to form a pair of gateposts.

South Zeal Cross

Location: SX651 935 (Near the chapel of St. Mary and St. Thomas).
Type: Village.
Trackway(s): None.
Height: Unattainable.
Span: Unattainable.
Circumference: Unattainable.
Alignment: North – South.
Comment(s): Possibly erected as a preaching station prior to the 18th century, the cross was repaired in the 1830s by a John Stanbury; he was a native of South Zeal on a return visit from America.
After completing the work, he carved his initials and the date on the base of the cross, but the locals took umbrage at this and erased the inscription. Incensed, John Stanbury returned to America vowing never to set foot in South Zeal again.

South Harton
- Cross at

South Zeal
Cross

Spurrell's Cross

Location: SX659 599 (South of Glasscombe Ball).
Type: Moorland.
Trackway(s): Plympton – Buckfast Monastic Way and the Blackwood Path.
Height: 1.74 metres.
Span: 43.5 centimetres.
Circumference: 93 centimetres.
Alignment: North – South.
Comment(s): The cross, also referred to as Purl's Cross in the past, was restored by the Dartmoor Preservation Association in about 1930, when it was re-erected on a new shaft. Prior to this the cross had become badly mutilated and its remains – the top portion of the shaft and only one arm – had, at some time, been placed in the midst of a small heap of stones.

Sticklepath – Inscribed Stone Near

Location: SX631 948 (On the right-hand side of the road leading from Sticklepath to Okehampton).
Type: Wayside.
Trackway(s): None.
Height: 1.27 metres.
Span: Not applicable.
Circumference: 98.5 centimetres.
Alignment: Not applicable.
Comment(s): The origins of this stone, believed to date from Saxon times, are unknown, but it has various inscriptions including, on its southern face, a circle cut in relief with incised radiating lines.

Sticklepath – Inscribed Stone Near

Spurrell's Cross

Stittleford's Cross

Location: SX742 760 (In the corner of the wall, 36 metres south of Hemsworthy Gate).
Type: Wayside.
Trackway(s): None.
Height: 14.5 centimetres (of incised cross).
Span: 15 centimetres (of incised cross).
Circumference: Not applicable.
Alignment: North-West – South-East.
Comment(s): This stone, also known as Stentiford Cross, is a boundary marker for the Manor of Dunstone. It has an incised cross and also carries the initials of Rawlin Mallock, an 18th century Lord of the Manor.

Swallerton Gate – Cross at

Location: SX739 791 (In the garden wall, facing the road).
Type: Wayside.
Trackway(s): None.
Height: 44 centimetres.
Span: 36 centimetres.
Circumference: Unattainable.
Alignment: North – South.
Comment(s): The origins of the cross, found in a nearby hedge in 1939, are unknown.

Stittleford's Cross

The Ten Tors Cross

Location: SX587 928 (About 90 metres north of Anthony Stile, inside Okehampton Military Training Camp).
Type: Moorland.
Trackway(s): None.
Height: 2.95 metres.
Span: 59 centimetres.
Circumference: 38 centimetres (tapered).
Alignment: West – East.
Comment(s): The cross has an inscription detailing its history, as follows: This cross was moved here in 1971 – from the original Ten Tors venue at Denbury camp – near Newton Abbot – It was presented in July 1960 to The Junior Leaders Regiment – Royal Signals by the people of Bovey Tracey to commemorate – the assistance given by their regiment at their – 700th Charter Anniversary celebrations – as the regiment had played a leading part in organising – the original and successive expeditions – When they left Denbury – they also left the cross and bequeathed it to – The Ten Tors Expedition.

Ter Hill Cross (West)

Location: SX641 706 (About 1.8 kilometres south of Swincombe Farm, on Ter Hill).
Type: Moorland.
Trackway(s): Buckfast – Buckland Monastic Way.
Height: 1.21 metres.
Span: 69 centimetres.
Circumference: 89.5 centimetres.
Alignment: North North-West – South South-West.
Comment(s): Erected on the 21st June 1994, and dedicated to the memory of the late Tom Gant (a well-respected Dartmoor personality), this cross is a replica of that currently on public display in the High Moorland Visitor Centre at Princetown.

A plaque on a nearby boulder reads: The Ancient cross here - was replaced in 1994 – in memory of Tom Gant – who loved Dartmoor. Ter Hill Cross (East) is visible from this location.

(The original cross was taken away in the interests of preservation as over the years it had been found recumbent and damaged on a number of occasions, probably as a result of animals rubbing against it, and had, eventually, become too fragile to remain on the open moorland)

Ter Hill Cross
(West)

Swallerton Gate
-Cross at

The Ten Tors Cross

Ter Hill Cross (East)

Location: SX642 706 (About 1.8 kilometres south of Swincombe Farm, on Ter Hill).
Type: Moorland.
Trackway(s): Buckfast – Buckland Monastic Way.
Height: 1.80 metres.
Span: 66 centimetres.
Circumference: 88 centimetres.
Alignment: North-East – South-West.
Comment(s): The cross was restored in 1885 and, unlike the original Ter Hill Cross (West), remains virtually undamaged.
Both Ter Hill Cross (West) and Skir Ford Cross are visible from this location.

Throwleigh – Cross at

Location: SX668 907 (Built into The Queen Victoria memorial in the village).
Type: Village.
Trackway(s): None.
Height: 91 centimetres.
Span: 62 centimetres.
Circumference: 82 centimetres.
Alignment: North-East – South-West.
Comment(s): The cross was restored and re-erected in 1897 to commemorate Queen Victoria's Diamond Jubilee. Its socket-stone had previously been used as a trough and is believed, originally, to have formed part of the churchyard cross.
In 1992 the plinth of the cross was struck by a vehicle, and during the subsequent repair work the cross was found to have been set in concrete. As a result, the Dartmoor National Park Authority used the opportunity to take away the cross for the purposes of removing the concrete and later re-erected it in a more appropriate type of mortar.

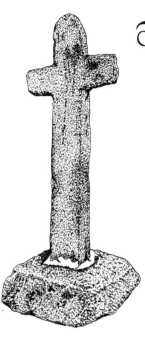

Ter Hill Cross
(East)

Throwleigh
- Cross at

Urgles Cross

Location: SX535 649 (Opposite the entrance to Urgles Farm on the right-hand side going uphill from the moorgate).
Type: Wayside.
Trackway(s): None.
Height: 2.06 metres.
Span: 55 centimetres.
Circumference: 91.5 centimetres.
Alignment: South South-West – North North-East.
Comment(s): A modern cross erected during the early part of the 20th century at the site of an ancient socket-stone that is now located in the grounds of Goodameavy House. Nothing is apparently known about the original cross.

Walkhampton – Cross at

Location: SX537 702 (On the verge opposite Church House and in front of the church).
Type: Village.
Trackway(s): Possibly Buckfast – Buckland Monastic Way.
Height: 2.01 metres.
Span: 64 centimetres.
Circumference: 93 centimetres.
Alignment: North-West – South-East.
Comment(s): The origins of the cross are not known, but for many years, up until 1976, the socket-stone and shaft were lying at the side of a nearby lane. In 1984, however, the socket-stone was moved to its present site and the shaft re-erected; in 1994 the head of the cross was replaced to complete the restoration.
The work was instigated and financed, initially, by the late Mrs. Helen Andrew, and it is interesting to reflect that Commander W. Andrew, who currently lives at Church House with his family, is the grandson of Lieutenant Malcolm Goldsmith R.N. (later to become Vice Admiral Sir Malcolm Goldsmith) – see Goldsmith's Cross.

Walkhampton
~ Cross at

Urgles Cross

Week Down – Cross on

Location: SX712 865 (About 1.5 kilometres south-east of Chagford on Week Down).
Type: Wayside.
Trackway(s): None.
Height: 1.94 metres.
Span: 47 centimetres.
Circumference: 1.345 metres.
Alignment: North North-East – South South-West.
Comment(s): In 1867 the cross was moved slightly as it was in danger of falling over. There is an incised maltese cross on the south-western face (22 centimetres high and with a span of 18 centimetres) and another incised maltese cross on the north-western face (24 centimetres high and with a span of 23 centimetres).

West Wyke – Cross at (Head Only)

Location: SX657 926 (South of the A30 and about 2 kilometres from South Zeal, at the entrance to the farm, under a large tree. Please note that this cross stands on private land).
Type: Wayside.
Trackway(s): None.
Height: 54 centimetres.
Span: 82 centimetres.
Circumference: 97 centimetres.
Alignment: Not applicable.
Comment(s): Nothing is apparently known about the origins of this cross and only the arms and part of the shaft remain.

West Wyke
- Cross at
(Head Only)

Week Down
- Cross on

West Wyke – Cross at

Location: SX657 926 (South of the A30 and about 2 kilometres from South Zeal, at the entrance to the farm, under a large tree. Please note that this cross stands on private land).
Type: Wayside.
Trackway(s): None.
Height: 1.42 metres.
Span: 44 centimetres.
Circumference: 1.3 metres.
Alignment: Not applicable.
Comment(s): For many years the cross was serving as a gatepost, but in 1958 it was removed and re-erected on its present site. There is an incised cross on the northern face (49 centimetres high and with a span of 33 centimetres) and another incised cross on the southern face (27 centimetres high and with a span of 27 centimetres).

The original gate-hanger holes are plainly visible.

Whealam Bottom – Cross at

Location: SX613 695 (About 730 metres south-east of Nun's Cross Farm).
Type: Wayside.
Trackway(s): None.
Height: 14 centimetres (of incised cross).
Span: 9 centimetres (of incised cross).
Circumference: Not applicable.
Alignment: North-East – South-West.
Comment(s): This stone is known as the 'Headless Cross' and it has been suggested that it is a boundary marker for the Southern and Western Quarters of the Forest of Dartmoor. The incised cross is on the north-western face.

Whealam Bottom
~ Cross at

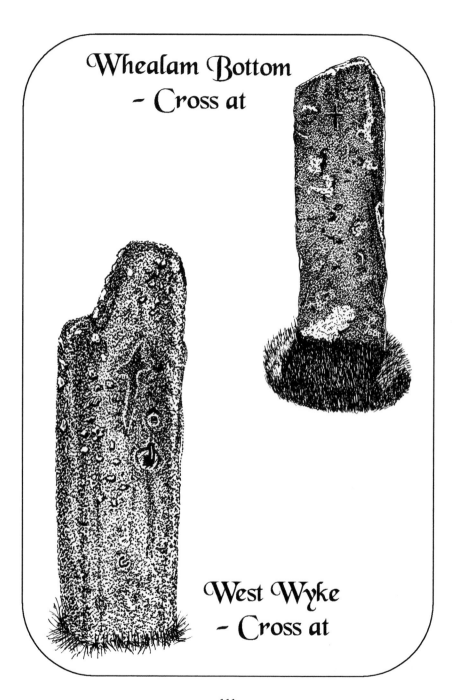

West Wyke
~ Cross at

Whitchurch Down – Cross on

Location: SX493 738 (West of Whitchurch Common Golf Course).
Type: Wayside.
Trackway(s): Buckfast – Tavistock Monastic Way.
Height: 1.21 metres.
Span: 62 centimetres.
Circumference: 1.14 metres.
Alignment: North-West – South-East.
Comment(s): The cross has been restored with the addition of a new shaft.

Widecombe-in-the-Moor – Cross at

Location: SX716 770 (At the entrance to the lane leading to Kingshead Farm from Natsworthy Valley Road).
Type: Village.
Trackway(s): None.
Height: 23.5 centimetres (of incised cross).
Span: 16 centimetres (of incised cross).
Circumference: Not applicable.
Alignment: North North-West – South South-East.
Comment(s): A gatepost with an incised cross, possibly once serving as a boundary marker.

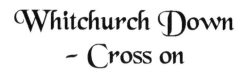

Whitchurch Down
- Cross on

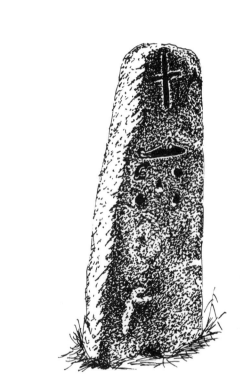

Widecombe-in-the-Moor
- Cross at

Widecombe Church – Cross at

Location: SX718 767 (In the churchyard, near the south porch of the church).
Type: Churchyard.
Trackway(s): None.
Height: 1.88 metres.
Span: 63 centimetres.
Circumference: 89 centimetres.
Alignment: West – East.
Comment(s):   The cross has been restored and has a replacement arm.

Widecombe Church – Crosses in

Location: SX718 768 (Inside the church on the left-hand side, by the door leading to the tower).
Type: Church.
Trackway(s): None.
Height: 68 centimetres (left-hand cross),
      68 centimetres (top cross),
      73 centimetres (right-hand cross).
Span: 25 centimetres (left-hand cross),
      30 centimetres (top cross),
      31 centimetres (right-hand cross).
Circumference: 45 centimetres (left-hand cross),
      58 centimetres (top cross),
      53 centimetres (right-hand cross).
Alignment: Not applicable.
Comment(s):   Found walled up in a staircase in the northern aisle. The top cross has an incised cross (15 centimetres high and with a span of 9.5 centimetres).

Widecombe Church - Crosses in

Widecombe Church - Cross at

Widgery Cross

Location: SX539 856 (On top of Brai (Brat) Tor).
Type: Moorland.
Trackway(s): None.
Height: Unattainable.
Span: Unattainable.
Circumference: Unattainable.
Alignment: North – South.
Comment(s):   The cross was erected in 1887 by the artist W. Widgery (father of F. J. Widgery) to commemorate Queen Victoria's Golden Jubilee. Also known as The Jubilee Cross, it is inscribed with 'W. Widgery, Fecit Jubilee VR'.

Windypost Cross

Location: SX534 743 (Northwards of Feather Tor, beside the Beckamoor Brook).
Type: Moorland.
Trackway(s): Jobbers' Road (Abbots' Way).
Height: 2.09 metres.
Span: 70 centimetres.
Circumference: 1.01 metres.
Alignment: West – East.
Comment(s):   Also known as Beckamoor Cross, this cross is believed to date back to the 16th century, or even earlier. The name Windypost almost certainly came about because of its exposed location.

Widgery Cross

Windypost Cross

Wrangaton Cross

Location: SX676 578 (On the roadside wall of a cottage, near the crossroads in the village).
Type: Village.
Trackway(s): None.
Height: 1.59 metres.
Span: 50 centimetres.
Circumference: 1.19 metres.
Alignment: North-West – South-East.
Comment(s): The cross was re-erected on its present site in 1959/60 after having previously stood in the grounds of Wrangaton House. Prior to that it had·been employed as a gatepost.

There is an incised cross on the north-eastern face (27 centimetres high and with a span of 23 centimetres) and another on the south-western face (25 centimetres high and with a span of 21 centimetres).

The cross also bears the following inscription: Victor Lobb – of Wrangaton – 1905-1977.

Yennadon Cross

Location: SX545 694 (Between the B3212 and Burrator road, at the crossroads on the left-hand side going uphill).
Type: Wayside.
Trackway(s): Buckfast – Buckland Monastic Way.
Height: 1.12 metres.
Span: 34 centimetres.
Circumference: 91 centimetres.
Alignment: North – South.
Comment(s): After having been built into a wall at Burham Farm at some time prior to the end of the 19th century, the cross was moved and re-erected on its present site in 1974.

There is an incised cross on the western face (14 centimetres high and with a span of 11 centimetres) and another on the eastern face (17 centimetres high and with a span of 13 centimetres), and there is evidence in the form of holes that the cross once served as a gatepost.

Wrangaton Cross

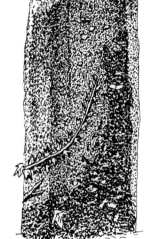

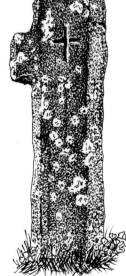

Yennadon Cross

The following is an assortment of crosses, or the remains of crosses, not included in the main section of this book:

Beatland Corner – Socket-stone at

Location: SX548 624 (On the roadside bank at the crossroads).

Comment(s): The socket-stone bears testimony to the fact that a wayside cross once stood at this location. However, nothing is known about the actual cross, or of its whereabouts.

The Bishop's Stone

Location: SX786 815 (By the roadside between the bridge and the road junction, near the old railway station).

Comment(s): This granite boulder is thought to be the pedestal of an ancient wayside cross. There are vague traces of a coat of arms incised on one face said to relate to either Bishop Grandisson (a 14th century Bishop of Exeter, who was supposed to have eaten a meal off the stone) or, possibly, Bishop Cotton of Exeter (1598-1621).

On another face of the boulder are the letters 'H C'; it has been suggested that this relates to Thomas Comyn, who was instituted to the living of Lustleigh Parish by Bishop Cotton in 1607.

Buckland-in-the-Moor – Pedestal of cross at

Location: SX720 731 (Just outside the south gate of the churchyard, surrounding a tree).

Comment(s): Nothing is known about the actual cross that would once have stood on this pedestal.

Coombe Tor – Cross on

Location: SX685 871 (On Coombe Tor. Please note that this cross stands on private land).

Comment(s): A comparatively modern cross erected in memory of a member of the Coniam family, who once owned the land. It carries the inscription 'M.A.L.C. 1908'.

Gidleigh Common – Cross on

Location: SX649 891 (At the foot of Kennon Hill, on its eastern side).

Comment(s): The boundary stone delineates the Gidleigh and Throwleigh parish boundaries and has an incised cross. It is also inscribed with the letter G (Gidleigh).

Greenwell Gert – Socket-stone at

Location: SX540 657 (On the roadside bank close to the tinners' gully on the north-western edge of Wigmoor Down).

Comment(s): This is another example where nothing is known about the actual cross.

Grimspound – Incised cross at

Location: SX701 809 (On the left-hand entrance post by the outer wall of Grimspound).

Comment(s): Nothing is known about this incised cross.

Hameldown R.A.F. Memorial Cross

Location: SX712 807 (About 1 kilometre east south-east of Grimspound).

Comment(s): The stone was erected in 1941 and has a small incised cross on its northern face, together with the following inscription: RAF – S49 – RDW – CJL – RB – RLAE – 21.3.41.
In 1991 the stone was re-dedicated and re-engraved, and a new plaque was placed on its southern face, which tells the full story: on 22nd March 1941 – a Royal Air Force Bomber – 49 Sqdn Scampton – crashed returning from – operations over France – the 4 crew were lost – this memorial bears – their initials and squadron – number – commemorating – their self-less courage – and that of fellow airmen – who perished on Dartmoor – 1939-1945 – their sacrifice helped us – to maintain freedom. – the Aircrew Association 1991

Hand Hill – Miniature cross on

Location: SX613 693 (On top of a large triangular boulder on the north-western slopes of Hand Hill).

Comment(s): This small brass cross is reputed to be the smallest cross on Dartmoor, although it now has some close contenders.
The cross, which first appeared in 1982, is also known as Northmore's Cross because it is thought to have been set up by some apprentices from Plymouth in memory of a member of the Northmore family.

Hanger Farm – Gatepost at

Location: SX612 587 (Near the entrance to Hanger Farm).
Comment(s): The gatepost is thought to be a mutilated cross and one that was never fully completed.

Lake Steep – Incised cross at

Location: SX705 725 (At the base of the wall beside the road leading up out of Poundsgate).
Comment(s): This incised cross serves as a memorial to a local doctor, who died nearby.

Meavy Church – Crosses at

Location: SX540 672 (On the outside of the church).
Comment(s): The large cross cut in relief over the south transept gable wall was an old tombstone that was found in a nearby hedge and dates back to around the 13th century. It was built into the present-day wall in 1825.
Nothing appears to be known about the three ancient crosses on the roof of the church.

Riddon Ridge – Incised cross on

Location: SX666 766 (On top of a boulder, which is about 45 metres north-east of the hut circle).
Comment(s): This incised cross may possibly be a waymarker for an old track leading to the Lich Way.

Skir Hill – Miniature cross on

Location: SX651 708 (On a small boulder amidst some small peat banks on the northern slopes of Skir Hill).
Comment(s): A small cross constructed from two nails. Its origin is unknown.

Sourton Green – Part of a shaft on

Location: SX534 903 (On the edge of the village green opposite The Highwayman Inn).
Comment(s): This shaft is the remains of the old village cross.

Sticklepath – Inscribed Stone at

Location: SX639 941 (Opposite Lady Well, on the roadside bank).
Comment(s): The origins of this stone are unknown, but it has various inscriptions (now undiscernible) and, on one side, a cross cut in relief.

Sticklepath – Cross at

Location: SX640 940 (On the roof of the Methodist Chapel, on the left-hand side of the road going towards Okehampton).
Comment(s): Nothing appears to be known about this old cross.

Teigncombe – Socket-stone at

Location: SX674 871 (In a gateway on the left-hand side of the road just before reaching the farm from the direction of Chagford).
Comment(s): It is thought that this is the base of a cross that may well have served as a waymarker for the ancient track known as the Mariners' Way.
The head of the cross was removed shortly after the beginning of the 20th century and mounted on a shaft of later date above Leigh Bridge.

Throwleigh Church – Shaft of cross at

Location: SX668 907 (In the churchyard to the left of the main path).
Comment(s): The shaft was found built into a wall at Throwleigh Barton and was erected at its present location by the Dartmoor National Park Authority in 1987. It is thought that it may be part of the original cross that would once have stood on the base currently situated in the centre of the village.

Traveller's Ford – Miniature cross above

Location: SX590 784 (At the base of a large black boulder that stands on the western slopes of the hill above Conies Down Water and the ford).
Comment(s): This small metal cross probably serves as a memorial, and there could be some significance in the fact that the Lych Way passes below this spot.

APPENDIX: LIST OF CROSSES
(In Map Grid Reference Order)

BIBLIOGRAPHY

Breton, The Rev. H. Hugh (1990) *Beautiful Dartmoor and its Interesting Antiquities.* Forest Publishing.

Breton, The Rev. H. Hugh (1990) *The Forest of Dartmoor.* Forest Publishing.

Crossing, William (1987) *The Ancient Stone Crosses of Dartmoor.* Devon Books.

Hemery, Eric (1983) *High Dartmoor.* Robert Hale Limited.

Hemery, Eric (1986) *Walking Dartmoor's Ancient Tracks.* Robert Hale Limited.

Masson Phillips, E. N. Various papers in the *Transactions of the Devonshire Association.*

Starkey, F. H. (Harry) (1989) *Dartmoor Crosses and some Ancient Tracks.* Published privately.

Thurlow, George (1993) *Thurlow's Dartmoor Companion.* Peninsula Press Ltd.

Watkins, Alfred (1995) *The Old Straight Track.* Abacus.

Woods, Stephen H. (1988) *Dartmoor Stone.* Devon Books.

Woods, Stephen H. (1996) *Widecombe-in-the-Moor.* Devon Books.

Reference has also been made to numerous Church Guides, as well as various issues of the *Dartmoor Magazine* (Quay Publications, Brixham) and *The Dartmoor Newsletter* (The Old Dartmoor Company).

THE AUTHOR

Tim Sandles was born in the Cotswolds town of Chipping Norton in 1957, and now lives in Denbury with his partner, Irene, and children. For the past 20 years or so he has worked in the agricultural industry as a sales representative specialising in animal medicines, and is currently employed in the Animal Health Merchant sector.

Tim has always had a great love of the countryside and most of the activities connected with it. Walking, in particular, has always played an important role in his life and, after moving to Devon in 1991, he quickly developed an interest in photography. This, in turn, led to a passion for exploring the wonders of Dartmoor and an ever-increasing desire to learn more about it, his knowledge having subsequently been enhanced by many letterboxing excursions and by the reading of numerous publications related to the moor.

Some 2 years ago, Tim's interests also led on to experimentation with pen and ink in order to produce drawings from his collection of photographs, in particular those depicting granite subjects – stone crosses were to prove to be his favourite! The process was very much on a self-taught basis, but the results achieved by Tim were such that he has been able to produce illustrations for *The Dartmoor Newsletter*, several T-shirt and sweatshirt designs, and now this, his first, book.

Tim Sandles